Root & Bone
Poems and Stories

by

Liz Baxmeyer

Finishing Line Press
Georgetown, Kentucky

Root & Bone
Poems and Stories

Copyright © 2024 by Liz Baxmeyer
ISBN 979-8-88838-808-2 First Edition
All rights reserved under International and Pan-American Copyright Conventions. No part of this book may be reproduced in any manner whatsoever without written permission from the publisher, except in the case of brief quotations embodied in critical articles and reviews.

ACKNOWLEDGMENTS

With appreciation to the editors of the journals who gave the following pieces first homes:

Beyond Words Literary Magazine: "Inosculation" (short fiction) and Sleeping Dryad (art)
Querencia Press's Not Ghosts but Spirits, Volume 1: "A Graft for Time" (poetry)
Lumiere Review: Ent Wife (art)
Moss Puppy Magazine: The Sanctuary Tree (art)
Typishly Literary Magazine: "Yowl" (short fiction)

Publisher: Leah Huete de Maines
Editor: Christen Kincaid
Cover Art and Design: Liz Baxmeyer
Author Photo: Miranda R. Carter

Order online: www.finishinglinepress.com
also available on amazon.com

Author inquiries and mail orders:
Finishing Line Press
PO Box 1626
Georgetown, Kentucky 40324
USA

Access to Audio Content:

Please use the password rootbone24 to access audio content

Contents

Earth Speak 1

Sleeping Dryad (Art) 2

Inosculation 3

Abscission 6

A Graft for Time 8

Rooting 9

The Queen of Trees 10

Ent Wife (Art) 11

Ent Wife 12

Ginny Greenteeth 13

Mendocino Man 14

Picture Window in Spring 15

The Sanctuary Tree (Art) 16

Wood Woman 17

Yowl 18

For Brynn

"We all have forests in our minds. Forests unexplored, unending. Each one of us gets lost in the forest, every night, alone."
—Ursula K. Le Guin, *The Wind's Twelve Quarters*

Earth-Speak

She called my name
once when I could not
find the words
or sounds,
only a scream
that I gave to the ground
that the earthworms heard
and carried
in dry-tongued pulses
to her roots;
                        a cacophony
                              of whispers.

Sleeping Dryad—Acrylic and mixed media on canvas

Inosculation

She was always there, swaying in the breeze, shielding me from the road beyond. She listened intently while I whispered my grievances like prayers through the glass and rain and the fizzing traffic beyond. She responded with a wave and bristle of her plush, emerald hair and told me, in a voice all rasp and wood, that it would take time before I would hear my own voice again.

I did not yet understand her meaning.

I was afraid the first time she spoke to me, her tone so unlike a human voice—deep and resonant like the sound of someone speaking though a broken underground pipe threaded with roots and lined with cracked metal or clay; a voice reclaimed by nature; a root through the throat; the acoustics of dirt. Earthworm-speak.

She told me her name was Bala of the Ilexes. She became my dryad.

Bala spoke to her brothers and sisters through the roots and silt. It was how she could see through far-away windows, like portals to other worlds: a bone-root network of vibrations sharing languages and stories. Sometimes the birds carried the dryads' messages, but they were often forgetful, unreliable, never translating the right words from heart to tongue.

She would tell me tales about strangers—the stories other trees told her: how the moles on Anthea's back were becoming misshapen but she still refused, even at her boyfriend's insistence, that she see a doctor. Instead, she prayed to her dryad for strength. Then there was the commotion Zoe created by burning the Easter meal because she found out her husband had been unfaithful and couldn't bring herself to tell anyone, except for her garden holly tree, whom she confided in the most. And then there was Milo, whose dryad was the great Oaken one, Hama, sheltered by the courtyard of St. Joseph's hospital one town over. Milo had been in a coma for weeks, unable to speak, except through the electric signals of his body. Only Hama understood him.

"There's something about how human bodies sing to trees that resounds like no other vibration," Bala said. "It is as if our species have a mutual understanding from before time. The human nervous system, if splayed out without its skin and bones, looks much like spindled branches, or an unfurled fern, but with large, round eyes that often see more than they can perceive." *Like a dryad.*

I asked of my family across the sea, but Bala could not speak nor hear through oceans. They were too chaotic, their walls protected by towers of salt and the deafening whispers of fish folk. The sound of wood deadened when it hit the water. Roots and twigs, she told me, could not permeate the seas. The salt dried and shriveled dryads' veins if they tried. "This is why the wind-warped cypress perpetually wretches over the cliffside. The salt is bitter and most sickening in her throat," she said.

She told me my voice sounded, to her, like a series of echoes and breathy vacuums vibrating against the window and into the ground, down through grubs and grass roots until it, or something made of it, reached her in flickers and fragments between the high whoosh and low rumble of the underworld. Her bark skin absorbed my fleshy undulations as she stood rooted to the spot. I told her how I had heard her from the earth, the feeling that shot up through my toes and into my body, the sound of rasping wood.

"We hear each other similarly, then" she said.

"What about Milo?" I asked. "How does Hama hear him when he cannot speak?"

She told me that dryads can hear not only words but the intentions and needs of the human body. "There's a vibration to your desperation, or desire, that resounds inside of me like nothing else" she said. "Even when your world is silent, I hear your longing."

I secretly visited those she told me about because knowing the intimate details of their lives weighed on my conscience. I wondered if they knew of me—my grief and conversations—through their own dryads. I watched through Anthea's window to see how misshapen her moles really were and wondered which part of knowing the truth she feared. I shopped at the same supermarket as Zoe when she dropped a large bag of rice and sobbed uncontrollably as it split like an atom and scattered into all corners of the aisle. I comforted her shaking body as a stranger. I tried to visit Milo but when the time came, I could not build the courage to enter the hospital.

Bala reminded me that it was not my place to intervene. It would cost me her kinship if I did, and I didn't want to lose it for the sake of my own guilt.

So, I chose to try and forget my knowledge.

But forgetting eventually sifted my soul, bit by bit, into a vacuum of rhythmic uncertainty until one day, I gave myself to it and stopped remembering anything at all.

My toes sprouted shoots and grew downward plunging into soft, black earth. My belly hardened and cracked and browned and my arms twisted upward, curling around my neck as my mouth filled with leaves and the soft down of baby birds. The world became a rustle of vibrations, and I heard the worms deliver their timeless incantation.

I heard my own voice.

Abscission

Perhaps it began when I miscarried the first time—
maybe the second—
maybe when my daughter was finally born and
could not sup milk without choking,
and turned blue in the lips
and stopped breathing
altogether.

> We had to learn to feed her another way,
> for my breasts were no longer safe;
> they rooted too deeply within her throat.

Perhaps it was when the elder tree fell to the ground,
leaving him unable to speak
after singing for centuries
about the glory of the sun's rays
as they split through ancient oak trees.

> He had to craft another voice—
> one quieter, more like the moon.

Perhaps it was when the willow tree
almost died from the great sickness
that invaded her trunk
like a fungus eating heartwood.

> After, small coils sprung from her head
> like tiny nests for tiny birds.

Or perhaps it was when my pleas to revive my first dog
fell silent against the edge
of an English forest
as it sucked my young voice
into a nearby sapling.

Now, the leaves fall from me more easily,
and each year as autumn coats my throat
with rotting foliage
I thank the forest for its opaqueness,
and let another branch drop
        like a broken wing
                from my
                        mouth.

A Graft for Time

I grafted a fleck of your jawbone to the root of a hawthorn tree.

You grew within its spindled branches,
and instead of alveoli, bore clusters of red berries;
instead of teeth, hard needles of umber
for protection.

When spring came, your tongue split into a million soft, white blossoms,
and you released them into the air;
a silent chorale drifting lightly
above the breeze.

Purple finches took refuge in the thickets of your lungs,
and in fresh nests of twigs and twine,
bore sweet and songful young
warbling tales of the tenderness and tenacity
of root and bone.

I grafted a fleck of your jawbone to the root of a hawthorn tree.
This way, they will call you sacred,
and never cut you down.

Rooting

I used to reach for the sun and grow almost instantly;
a constant thirst quenched abundantly by wonder.
Each finger would form a new branch;
on each tooth, shoots with pungent blossoms and light green leaves;
ears spiraling inward forming sweet, twisted coils of twine
where birds would nest and sing.

Now, the growing happens much more slowly
because I question every inch of it
and ask the sun why I get to rise
and become a haven for small creatures
while others do not.

Sometimes, I wonder why I must change
when I am quite happy as I am,
even if, in the end,
I know some revelation will likely come.

Sometimes, I try to abstain from growth altogether
because I am tired of the process;
tired of the grace it requires
to explore the cracks and splinters of something new,
or to unearth fresh truths: the very roots of living.

Finding them leads to untruths that fester like dry rot,
and the world is adorned with so many well-crafted lies.

How should I prepare my daughter for this part of growing?
She extends herself so quickly toward the stars that I sometimes wish
I could make a spell to keep her three-years-old for just another year,
long enough for her to let her own roots settle
in her feet and brain, and on her tongue;
enough for her to understand what it means to abstain from growth;
to pause;
to sit in lichen until winter icicles sing
under threaded branches once more.

Who am I to govern where her roots should travel?

The Queen of Trees

On the path to Wenlock, I met the Queen of Trees. I bowed at her introduction, and when she extended a fingered branch adorned with fragrant apple blossoms, I kissed it on cue, as any mortal person would. She asked whence I hailed and I told her, with trembling jaw—for I was so in awe of her splendor—"I am of this place, like you." I do not think she knew me, fleshy and weak as I was, but she offered to walk with me to the edge of the forest in exchange for my company and conversation—for trees are often thirsty for news of the land. We spoke about the things our hearts and minds desired in common: silence, reverent love, a forever morning resounding with birdsong, fresh spring water. When we reached the other side she kissed me on the cheek and whispered, in a voice all rasp and wood, "Do not forget this Queen of Trees, for my roots are within you, and one day you shall need me more than you know."

I breathed deeply, and followed the open sky home.

Ent Wife—Acrylic and mixed media on canvas

Ent Wife

She lays out her daily tasks
allocating a limb
or finger
to each.

A spindled branch will become
a scribe to write lists;
a weaver of baskets;
a conductor of breezes.

Her twisted roots—
now limber from being stretched
and contorted
over and over
like the tendons of an accordionist—
are piled loosely at the base of her trunk
allowing her to move from the way
of falling leaves
or lovers who might carve their names
on her strong, bark-roughened torso.

She is both marked and unmarked
by the passing of time—
a sentinel, a mother of birds, a crone,
in the midst of others
who would share their earth,
their stories and roots:
the very sustenance of their being,
and sup ground water together
from deep earthen wells.

So, she becomes,
and sings with wood-resounding voice
to the day, and the day, and the day,
until the birds no longer nest
in her ears
and on her aged bones.

Ginny Greenteeth

Many years ago, I fell into the grasp of Ginny Greenteeth—when she was young and ruled the forest with abominable acts. The birds avoided the pond where she resided; foxes would not drink from it, even in great thirst, for fear of being dragged under by her claw-like hands. Children would run away screaming, for if they peered into it too long—usually for a dare set upon them by friends—she would tug at their clothing to warn them not to linger. She was always hungry. When defied by some brave beast, which was rare, she would become (as is true to her name), green with rage. Her wrath would cover everything in a thin film of algae and moss until creatures, and even trees, became paralyzed with fear and slickened with clay and deadly skullcap. To punish travelers unfortunate enough to have to sleep in her domain, she would claw out of the gloomy waters, belly down, clutching at sod and rocks, and cast a foul and deathly breath upon their innocent, resting faces; they would awaken, buried under soil and blinded by ravenous earthworms.

I was taken into her vile, brown water while cooling my face, ignorant to her presence at the time, but was fortunate to be saved by a majestic young deer whose antlers fished me out, impaling Ginny Greenteeth's snake-like arm and steeping her waters in emerald-grey blood.

A lifetime later, I still expel the silt from my lungs, and it will take a good while longer for my heart to squeeze her dark magic from its ventricles.

Mendocino Man

Out in the Western redwoods
just north of Mendocino
there lives a man;
more, the essence of a man—
a ghost of memory and of time.

He stands tall alongside his siblings,
the intricate bones of their feet intertwined.
Some are broken with age and set in strange shapes,
but they hold, tall as they are.
His neck stretches
into the hazy opaqueness of northern sky;
a blind sentinel, protector of high places.

This giant of time
in a grave of moss and wood
sees just far enough above the horizon
to always sense what is coming.

Picture Window in Spring

Beyond the veil of glass
the small garden tree,
now laden with shades of spring,
sways slightly in
a whisp of breeze.

I think about
how that spindled creature
looked last year
and how I suppose I haven't
paid enough attention
because it seems
the same to me now
as it did then,
though it's probably fuller
and more accepting of life.

We often assume beautiful things
will sustain themselves
because their beauty allows them the privilege
when it will not,
and it is easy to ignore when
things continue to grow into their beauty—
even through great trauma or revelation.
That is often how it works
when we start to heal,
and sometimes when we don't.

This is how we know we can turn back into trees.

The Sanctuary Tree—acrylic and mixed media on canvas

Wood Woman

The Wood Woman had a baby in the wildflower clearing. All alone, she pushed the little earthen creature out, writhing and cursing her way through the deep, relentless pain. A white hare stared at her through bluebells and grasses with an expression of both whist and disbelief. When she had delivered the child, she sat breathless in a warm, shallow river on a bed of sand and pyrite passing the placenta, dipping her fingers in the water to wet the crying babe's brow and clean off what remained of the womb. Euphoric and bone-weary, she rested in contentment, yet, knew wolves would smell the scent of birth and come stalking them in the night.

She chanted a lullaby which held the truth to elation and grief, all in one.

The hare did not move, even an inch.

Yowl

We had moved from the city into Ione Farmhouse in the dead of the first COVID summer, the pine trees already crisp with that other California fever. The house itself, painted a powdery blue and wrapped in twisted, browning ivy sat like a lick of freshness on top of a small brush-covered bluff, our nearest neighbors about a half a mile down to one side and out of sight. The heat pressed down in pulses, and everything moved with it; even the gold-dirt track leading to the place swayed like a rattlesnake during the hottest hours. Sometimes whisps of burn could be seen drifting up into the empty, cobalt sky; I guess we were lucky to have just missed the fires that year.

Now we are under a different kind of hard brightness; still, dank, foggy, frozen by walls of time. From a distance the property looks much like a snow globe you'd pick up in a holiday gift store with its glistening lane, the snow revolving around it in whispers the only thing moving. Inside this world there is another vista.

Marybelle arrives halfway through the winter, pink and warm against the backdrop of freeze: a welcome disturbance to these silent wilds.

She cries a lot at first. We feed the furnace to keep her cozy as she sups milk for comfort, hour upon hour, but she is restless in sleep and wakes suddenly, my pulse and my breast quick to react. I sleep with her on the rug in the living room for the first month; Ben consigns himself to the couch. We live as if in some kind of deep-safe hibernation. Feed. Sleep. Cry. Sing. Cry. Sleep. Sing. We cycle through trying to find the magic spell to restful. I feel like we never really get there, at least, not until we find the abandoned female tabby kitten sleeping in an old Singer box in the derelict barn down the lane—her mother likely taken by a fox or coyote.

We name her Bobbin. She is drawn to Marybelle and seems to be able to calm her the most; more, even, than my lullabies and soothing motherly hushes. We live for months in this zoetrope.

***

At two-years-old, Mary-bee—the name she earns for the sound she makes in her sleep—is quieter. She doesn't say much, though we know she can. Her doctor puts it down to shyness and an overactive imagination keeping her inside her mind often. She doesn't see many people, aside from quick trips to the store or brief visits from busy family she can't get to know well in such haste. She thinks most people live inside a computer screen because that's how Ben and I work much of the time. The psychologist we were referred to says it's mild anxiety, likely just a phase related to age and isolation. I question whether we should have moved away from the city, from parks and play dates and family—during the height of a pandemic—to raise our baby. Our attempt at an uncomplicated, quiet life has caused our child to move inward. She speaks to Bobbin, though, in soft purrs and mews, sometimes in full, cat-chatter-like sentences. They chitter back and forth in abstract conversation; it's sweet, though increasingly, perhaps worryingly, constant. The cat is full grown now, sleek and majestic in her own way. I am glad we found her, despite the fact our daughter cannot detach; she seems to need more family than we can give.

***

Spring comes. She is three now. We work the tangled yard for the first time in a year; the roses need trimming from the windows and the ground tilling for large weeds; we like to keep the garden a little chaotic, knowing where we are, and let the smaller weeds grow if the butterflies like them. Bee seems ready to explore more freely within the bounds of the property. We don't yet know this is the beginning of something.

As the days keep more light, we lose her to the woods and grasses for hours. This is not something that was agreed, but it starts to happen more, and we are powerless against it. I worry at first. Ben does not fully accept this amount of freedom for our girl at such a young age. But Bobbin attends to her, fierce as a lynx; we've seen how she wards off raccoons and I tell him this is a different life we have chosen. This life is good for our daughter's soul—nature is nothing for her to fear. It is why we moved here, after all. The two always return home and are ravenous for meat and water.

Bee speaks less, so I adopt a kind of body language that mirrors hers; a way of moving that lets her know I understand, and that gesture is enough. Meanwhile, I read on how to bring her back, if I can; she is acting more animal than human, and yet, she is still more human than many. I see no great strangeness in how she is and feel guilty for even thinking of betraying it with literature or medicine. One morning, she catches a House Martin and leaves it on the dinner table as an offering. I think it's Bobbin's at first till I see the blood on the corner of Bee's mouth. I cannot not bring myself to be angry at such a gut-savvy and fiercely sweet gesture; I have never been inclined to perpetuate the idea that girls must be graceful, not this unique and wild creature of mine, so fiercely present in the world. Still, I treat her for the possibility of parasites just the same.

One night, close to summertime, Bobbin is killed by a fox and left with slick entrails out in a corner of the garden. I am terrified for my Bee; for her body and heart. I keep her inside at night from now on, but she yowls incessantly at the window, a strange song of human sobs and feline screams, grieving her furred sister. Her first real trauma. I try to comfort her with soft strokes and chin bumps, the way Bobbin would have. She is not wholly appeased.

Ben is sicker with worry than me. He feels she is moving too far into the unknown; he is losing his little girl. She's like me, I say. I tell him she dreams of the trees and the goose grass and needs to feel their touch, rub her skin against bark. It's how she knows the world is real. It's how she makes her mark. He cannot fathom it, and after time I begin to worry more, too. This state that was once playful now seems dangerous and primal, like it's a place she will enter into too deeply and not return, not even to the most distinctive Bee parts that I cherish.

***

At four-years-old, she will no longer tolerate the forty-minute car ride to see the psychologist.

She mews loudly in the early hours; scuttles around the house after a spider or loose bead. I hear her scratch incessantly at doors she cannot open, and call with a hopeless high-pitched whine, but Ben will no longer let her in our bedroom at night, not when she's like this. He is frightened. Last time she frenzied, he cracked the door and in a flash of nail and tooth she drew blood from his index finger; he pulled it back, dripping red, and slammed the door shut. They both cried hard that night: his, a grown man's whimper—hers, the bitter yowl of a cat. The next morning, she purred softly and rubbed her cheek against his until her guilt was relinquished by his embrace, and they let the vibrations of her incantation heal them both.

I am rooted to her, though I cannot say I do not fear her will.

By the next winter, Ben leaves us. He cannot accept the way we choose to live—it is too maddening. The grief is too hard, and he cannot not bear what he cannot fix. He cannot bear that she is no longer his soft, cherry-cheeked little girl—an innocent babe who does not know death. I see now that that isn't what she needs to be, so, when she decides it is time, I give her back to the forest. I leave offerings of toys and milk for her to claim when the day brightens, and sometimes I hear her crying in the night—this creature I mothered into the wild.

Liz Baxmeyer is a writer, artist, musician, sound designer, composer and lecturer living in Northern California. She was born in Los Angeles to English and Cypriot-American parents but grew up in the English countryside where she learned about folklore and its connection to natural landscapes. In her teens, Baxmeyer was an avid painter, writer, and musician. She continued to compose music and songs and performed at various folk festivals across the UK. She went on to study music at the University of Wales, Bangor (now Bangor University) and earned an MA in music concentrating in music for media and the arts, and electroacoustic composition.

After leaving college, Baxmeyer moved back to California. She taught English and music classes at a college in San Francisco for six years while maintaining a career as both a touring singer-songwriter and sound designer/composer for bay area theatre productions, for which she earned eight nominations and two industry awards for sound design.

In 2017 Baxmeyer relocated to the Sacramento region and started lecturing at a health sciences university where she still works as full-time faculty in the humanities. In early 2023, she earned an MFA in Writing and Contemporary Media from Antioch University, Santa Barbara. Currently, Baxmeyer is undertaking a PhD in Creative Research at Transart Institute, working in the realms of sound, ecology, health, and reflective writing practices.

Baxmeyer has been published in a variety of literary outlets including *Beyond Words Literary Magazine*, *Wild Roof Journal*, *Syncopation Literary*, *The Examined Life Journal*, *Querencia Press*, *Typishly Literary Magazine*, *Luna Station Quarter*ly, and more. Her academic contributions can be found in IWAC proceedings, and NCTE. She presents regularly at conferences on the topics of creative research, audio pedagogies for writing and expression, and more. She is Founding Editor-in-Chief of *The Calendula Review: A Journal of Narrative Medicine*.

Root & Bone is Baxmeyer's first chapbook and represents years of study and practice across disciplines. In this short volume, she combines poetry, art, and short fiction on themes that are consistently important to her creative work: the environment, folklore, feminism, and trauma.

www.ingramcontent.com/pod-product-compliance
Lightning Source LLC
Chambersburg PA
CBHW040308170426
43194CB00022B/2945